for Martha and Molly

SHEDDING SKIN

James Martyn

ARLEN
HOUSE

Shedding Skin

is published in 2010 by
ARLEN HOUSE
an imprint of Arlen Publications Ltd
PO Box 222
Galway
Phone/Fax: 353 86 8207617
Email: arlenhouse@gmail.com

Distributed internationally by
SYRACUSE UNIVERSITY PRESS
621 Skytop Road, Suite 110
Syracuse, NY 13244–5290
Phone: 315–443–5534/Fax: 315–443–5545
Email: supress@syr.edu

ISBN 978–0–905223–65–0, paperback
(a signed and numbered limited edition is also available)

Typesetting ¦ Arlen House
Printing ¦ Brunswick Press
Cover Image ¦ Pádraic Reaney

CONTENTS

7   My Father Grows Young
8   On Seeing Jim and Nora on the Beach at Agia Galini,
    Crete
9   Bachelor
10 Just in Time
11 Backdoor
12 Vagaries
13 Affaire
14 Apnoea
15 Night-Watchman
17 Retirement Plan
18 Under the Skin
19 Planter
20 Little Known Facts about Dancing
21 'New' Time
22 Non-Hollywood Days
23 Reverse Chronologist
24 Morning Jam
25 Hungry Man
26 'Good Seeing'
27 Tense
28 First Curse
29 Country Ways
30 Teacher
31 Beach in a Box
32 Off the Game
33 Black Earth
34 Hungry Woman
35 Dernier Cri
37 That Face
38 Fixation
39 Carving a Sheela na Gig
40 Recipe for Cooking a Hat
42 Cold Fever

43 Picturing the Frog
44 Away Too Long
46 How Ordinary he Looked
47 Lesson
48 The Mirror Thing
49 Second Curse
50 Stiltwalker
51 Spring
52 The Properties of Water
54 Worn Down
55 November Days
56 Warshow
57 Third Curse: Shedding Skin
58 Winter
59 Election-Time, Salthill
60 God in Tennis
61 Off the Motorway
62 History Lesson
63 Windfalls

64 About the Author
   Acknowledgements

MY FATHER GROWS YOUNG

The week he died my father grew young again,
his faculties returning in all their glory,
his hearing sharp to our conversations,
his sight picking out the trees along the ridge field,
his food tasting new and very fresh,
his harrowed limbs loosening and supple,
his fingers spry once more and full of tunes.
He gripped the fiddle neck with returned ease,
the strings pinging close to his delicate ear,
the bow leaping in his easy hand,
his arm angling to the music's climb,
his eyes focused on the inner notes,
his foot light to the steady rhythm,
returned images tripping off his tongue:
a helicopter static above a cornfield,
the first big diesel to run the line,
stuttering warplanes way off course,
the British forces leaving for home,
the terror of the news from France,
'NO POPE' scrawled on the Titanic,
his own mother's face when she was happy.

ON SEEING JIM AND NORA ON THE BEACH AT AGIA GALINI, CRETE

They drifted back from the beach bar
where we'd seen them earlier sharing a frappé,
he had the same dark spectacles perched,
his hair slicked back, the moustache neatly trimmed,
Nora looking Junoesque wrapped in a swirling towel.
He held the sun-bed attentively for her
until she sank into it, the full of her,
her kiss strangely red, touching him there
and there. He was reading a Grisham novel, I think,
when the incident occurred, the boombox
far too loud, the teenagers deaf to his pleas
for quiet, the bleached kid with the razor-cut
giving him the finger.
But, none of us
were prepared for what happened next, Jim
assuming the fireplace pose, left arm resting,
his right hooked into his beachwear as he launched
into 'Those Lovely Seaside Girls', his tenor
matching the scratching beats, his voice growing,
arms expanding to the full-power notes,
the boombox drowned as in a wave,
all the sun-tanned masses stilled,
transfixed by his final cut-glass thrill,
Nora's whispered, 'That's my Jim'.

BACHELOR

Midnight,
and the wheeling
chill-white moon,
eye-ball big
in the blind black sky
lights his way
by dark boreen and bog,
past neighbours held
in hatred and lust
and longing ache,
to closed-in path
and barking dog
and muddy underfoot,
to peeling door
and darkness
and no-one waiting
by the end window.

JUST IN TIME

When the man from the power company called
to advise on slipping our cables underground,
word was already abroad in our small community
that his light was fading. Something dark
was gripping him while he explained
about the minimum depth for burial,
stressed the care required when digging,
advised on the conduit to lay, grimaced
over the uneven ground, paced out the length
involved, braced himself for the hilly bits,
confided as he kicked our rotting poles,
gingerly, how they were almost gone,
how we'd phoned him – just in time.

BACKDOOR

Our old backdoor was pockmarked,
paw-marked, boot-marked, scuffed,
shouldered by greatcoated men,
calloused by their hands,
grated by the haggard winds
blistered by infrequent suns
cracked and cooled by sheeting rain,
its closing was a sudden slap
a ringing shut, a settling of accounts.

In sixty-three the house came down,
that door then went to block a gap,
decayed, a crust, which faded
to a shadow on the ground.
Digging out the back today,
at dusk I heard that sound again,
the sudden slap of pockmarked wood,
felt their ghosts in greatcoats
stride out between the muffled trees.

VAGARIES

There is a spell towards the end of March
when the angle of the earth and the spinning sun,
with the light refracted through the crowning sky,
the humours of the builders and the materials employed,
along with the casting of the panes and the imponderables
of the spheres conspire to blind the birds
to the invisible vagaries of glass.
One plump dove left a perfect angel imprint
on our kitchen window,
the beak, breast and claws, each feather,
and each barb of each feather outlined,
while the crow met the front-door panes
head-on, snapping his neck,
leaving him upended in the drain,
his plumage dulled, his claws unclasped,
his frozen eye refracting light.

AFFAIRE

That was the summer she felt him slipping
away, across the hills, scorched and bare,
to some new bedroom, rose-rounded,

no longer singing her favourite song.
She guessed it in his busy stare,
his sundrifted dreaming by the window,

the rising hill behind their house,
filling there, like a breast, peaking
to a newness in his unfocused eyes.

She tried harder then, entwining
herself around everything he did,
hurried touches on his cooling skin,

coy murmurings in crowded bars,
slow glances between them,
new dawns on their blue ceiling.

Yet that summer she felt him slipping,
a vagueness in his sheltered eyes;
his faintest humming of a new song,

the notes foreign to her vigilant ear.

APNOEA

Once they would have blamed the gods,
but now it's called prevailing weather.
Conditions which in the night
lowered an opaque cowl about us all
and we awoke to a thick soup
just beyond the harbour wall,
so close we could stir it.
Except that no boats sailed,
yet all day engine sounds
prevail and sometimes a craft
will barely break the grey skin
before entering its tendrils
again. The locals shake their heads
and count the fishing boats tied up
and listen closely to the sounds.
'Apnoea' they say and point it out:
our whole world in a bowl,
all breath held as in a dive;
and we sophisticates lie in the oven heat
and breathe the heavy pearled air,
aliens, fighting back the nagging
fear, that all, maybe, is not as we suggest,
the opaque bowl, the ghost sounds and the rest.

NIGHT-WATCHMAN

Out of the barrel of a gun he shot,
off to Canada in '22, cap down,
his eyes hidden from the boatman,
his collar up against the Catholic cold,
card-board coffin in his hand,
brown-belted, holding his few clothes
and a trilby hat, the one he wore
the cold-comfort night he found her out,
the gun under her chin,
the hammer cocked to her whispered 'no'.

Never settled after that, night-watchman,
he moved between darkness and the day,
his own man only, all debts covered,
the hungry eye seeing far and near.
Returned in '33 to a foreign state,
with the part-time gunmen all checked out,
cowboy soldiers owning land, murder replaced
with the civility of cracked heads.

An outsider now, he stayed with the dark,
sleeping through the business day, blossoming
to card games and tipped drinks, the cardsharps
knowing the hotel where he worked,
outsiders all, raking big pots in lean times.
Few people knew the one room
where he slept, kept the cardboard suitcase
packed beside his good shoes, believed they were
the secret to a suit, that and the double pants.

Smoking forty a day, he shunned tipped,
used a holder instead,
seldom mentioned the hard times
except when he was sober,
never used the gun again, but kept it oiled,
told the priest he preferred God wholesale,

he had little time for middlemen.
Imploded in a month, he covered his own burial,
a chorus of painted ladies filled the morgue.
Battening down the lid, I checked the loads,
slipped the oiled gun by his hand.

RETIREMENT PLAN

I will see you always crossing Quay Street,
no working clothes, scraped clean of purpose,
your too new crombie a neatly buttoned shroud.
From window to window, measured pace,
price-spotting, you store up conversation.
Later in the pub you'll tell half-truths
half-learned, to eyes focused just beyond you.
You'll drink two glasses, slowly, and linger
until the endless ache bewilders.
'Busy day tomorrow', then you'll leave,
no cutting-cruel discussion when you've gone.

Outside in the doorway of some vacant shop
you'll smoke that other borrowed cigarette,
while litter-eddies gambol at your feet.
Collar clasped, you'll read the torn sky,
hoping someone talks about the weather.
No one comes. The cars hiss by with purpose.
The busker Dylans 'in the wind' as you ghost by,
seeing your shadow lengthen and another dead day die.

UNDER THE SKIN

An arm rammed in the tube-train doors,
his ragged rage-voice proclaiming:
'they'll stop for me!' with its years
of nurture mapped out on his face,
the platform slowing from its seething
spin, eyes averted, his Asda bag of tins
clattering the frame, his friends hauling him
back with promises of the next one,
the next train, promises he's heard for years
without delivery, bosses mauling him,

while always there 'behind the lines', the drink,
spirit-boots to suck him down and down again,
to a docket-book of cheap digs, a riffle-run
of peeling kips, down then to doorways,
piss-clean, until there was only this:
his arm wedged, the underground held back,
restrained, the faded tri-colour, where it bulged
below the elbow absorbed, back into the skin,
but holding-on none the less, giving nothing
to the Brits but pain, even if it was his own.

And it would come to him again: roused up
to Easter Sunday mornings, with songs
of Garryowen, 'Ireland's Holiest Day',
his father called it. Squeezed into the car
and driven to the seashore facing Wales,
released onto the washed sand and urged
to gather them in, 'to leave the round ones,
to pick them good and sharp', his Easter
mornings spent throwing stones at England.

PLANTER

'... At a more minor key, homesickness and nostalgia
are also Honeysuckle states'

– The Twelve Healers and Other Remedies

He told me that it was an elm tree,
how the elms were dying everywhere
but mine was looking healthy and alive.
Produced three small honeysuckle shoots,
and planted them to climb the lilac bush,
then he walked amongst the weeds,
naming them as winter heliotrope,
it had haunted my corner for years
and offered competition as a cure:
fresh grass would kill it off, drive it
underground. Explained to me how
he was a planter who'd come west,
met his wife on a forest path while
looking for new challenges, raised
a family, all scattered to the winds,
spent his time now finding patches
of old woodland lost among the pines,
believed these places were for saving,
new battles to be fought. How his wife
had died, but her plants kept him going,
how she'd loved her growing things.
He'd bring her slips from off the shrub,
and she'd nurse the saplings, talking
to them like friends, feeding them,
her green-stemmed children, lulling
them to fullness and how this care
had filled their garden. He missed her.
The honeysuckle evening brought her
back, wild woodbine around him now,
he would fill the world with her scent.

LITTLE KNOWN FACTS ABOUT DANCING

The pot-oven in the posh antique shop
had embossed arms, lion-claw legs,
with a regal, posing lion astride the lid.
I was reminded of its country cousin
inverted before the cottage hearth
submerged there in the gritty soil,
an echo chamber for the dancers' heels,
the lilter mouthing in the dark,
the hurtling swing of heavy skirts,
bodies whirling to the battered reels.

Or the famine house in Mayo
renovated lately by a dancing man
who raised the flaggy hearth
in the hope of finding a rusting pot,
but found instead twelve horses' heads
set semicircle 'round the fire,
their skulls a sounding chamber
for the dancers' feet,
their sockets clogged with the red clay,
its flint hardness all that remained
of the dancers' beat.

'NEW' TIME

My father drove out wintertime
from the height of a kitchen chair,
reaching up to move the big hands
on, a baker's dozen of chimes
filling the house with time; midnight
passes in a stroke pushing us
forward to a new day, mother
testing all our patience for weeks
'til she no longer felt the need
to give the time 'another day'.
The clock settled to its new task,
the drop of the big weights steady,
the pendulum and the echo,
neighbours turning in new-lit fields,
all our evenings stretched with light.

NON-HOLLYWOOD DAYS

Some days the sirens just barely weep,
or the dust-drenched cars sweep past,
the officers knocking on the wrong door,
pinning some other suspect to the tiles,
while the elevator opens on a tableau
involving no violence, gun crime or
grievous harm. On days like that, work
just happens: you get home untroubled
by blondes or brunettes of any gender,
slow-cruising cars with darkened glass
ease up to some other kerb, no-one
hands you the black bag, the laptop
with the retinal recognition codes, or
the missing pulse of the suitcase bomb.

The only eyes you meet are in the bathroom
mirror, you know Moses is out there frozen
on the wrong mountain, the golden ticket
has faded in the wash, the dia-lithium crystals
are on another bus, while the naked alien
crashes to earth by some distant fence.
Even old 'Sing it Sam' has the night off,
the piano lying there, useless, an APB
out for the lost chord. However, these are
the blear days shaping real heroes,
the bruised ones who haven't read the script,
will never ever get to be word perfect.

REVERSE CHRONOLOGIST

It fascinates me, this excavation of the news,
treating each year like some major dig;
stacking your newspapers in towers of time,
until one day, just past the turn of a season,
you ease into your reading chair and begin
working back and back from a chosen present
where everything is full and new. The news
surprising you with its broadness before

you start to pare it down and narrow it,
as you turn the pages, back through time,
much becoming useless as you sift,
items falling away, becoming sops or spin,
small particles of dust to brush aside,
the major bodies standing out – planets,
obvious from the dross, calling to you
for exploration, for some further time.

And I imagine you arriving at the final
page of the final paper, already knowing
almost all which is contained there,
having burrowed through the stacks,
you trawl its histories, searching
for the few shards, the lodestones
which have led you back and back,
meeting moons which wane and slowly wax.

MORNING JAM

Holding on at the white line,
the uphill dash all fume and mist,
tyre hiss and the lift of gears,
trucks pushing outwards, labouring,
trailer-loads of sand, metal bars,
bound for foundations and dark
work, a mother clinging to the wheel
with a Mexican-wave of children
in an SUVee, behind a cow in a trailer,
suspicious, eyeing a box-van of pork
products, the driver, white-coated,
a surgeon going right for the hospital,
nurses shuffling home, the groan
of a Guinness truck, metal-tuned,
finding purchase for the long haul,
with a hornet-flight of bikes, gnat-
angry through the crawling grid,
a carriage-line of cars all wiper-swipe,
with side-lamps glowing, business
people groomed and suited for the day,
a battery of lights, a flash. I slot in.

HUNGRY MAN

Teenaged at a time when sex was exotic,
a spice carried on the wind across the Irish Sea,
you cut the process short by concentrating your energies
on Sunday communicants; spying on the regulars
who confessed on Saturdays their doings of the week,
telling us, the confused ones, there was a link
between their confessing and the need,
surmising their trips to the darkened box
were linked to other deeds in cinema seats and alleyways.
You stalked them then, fixing their faces,
your knee bent to the confessional door,
the rest of us huddled on tormented corners
as you swept past escorting some girl
with her hungers gauged, our jealousy burning
like sin, but admiring your ingenuity;
your ability for thinking outside the box.

'GOOD SEEING'

'It's all in the focus', the starman said,
as we stood in the clear-as-crystal dark,
nothing between us but the tripod scope,
his eye pressed to the shiny metal piece,
feeling out to the farthest of the stars
in minute steps of calibrated touch.

'What you're seeing here is *look back time*,
it's coming to you now from long ago',
and he'd straighten to peer into the sky,
while I would lean into the silver disk
to see that world beyond the naked eye,
suspended there in the 'good seeing' air.

'Scintillation!' he'd bellow, 'puts us off',
his breath a cloudy column in the dark;
explaining how the air bends the starlight,
causing it to twinkle, this was *bad seeing*.
'Always beware bad seeing', he would say,
his telling even more than he could know.

Once he told me the tale of *Baily's Beads*,
how one should never meet the sun head-on,
how old astronomers would smoke a glass
to help observe the sun's worshipped eclipse.
'Just sunlight gleaming through the moon's high peaks',
plain honest light must still be taken slow.

Umbra and penumbra were *eclipse* words,
cones of shadow reflected on the earth,
leaving parts in darkness and others bright,
explaining how what existed was the same,
only each one's point of view was changed
to take us from the shadow into light.

TENSE

We were working through the tenses,
practising the swing from present
to past. Seeing how you could take
the future as anticipation of the 'now',
even if it fills our days with the most
dread, it is still easily learned.
We stood in the back garden observing
the dusk conveyor-belt towards us;
the shadow swing of the saplings
by the wall, the individual drop
of the blossom, the singular beat
of the gull craving towards the shore,
while you practised, reciting your litany:
from running to ran and trying to tried,
from doing to did and walking
to walked, while the daylight closed
around us; the skeletal apple-tree
shadowing over the grass,
until there was only the voices
of the children playing hide and seek
and you had whispered, going ... gone.

First Curse

The hill will be steep and slippery with doubts,
your scattered pearls of certainty turning underfoot
like shale. You will climb alone,
those you know seeing you off from base-camp,
happy to be turning back, skipping nimbly
aside to avoid your loosened scree.

The sun will be hot, the sky a burning wall.
The birds will be black and crying.
There may be wolves and the cave,
if you find one, will be cold,
the mouth blocked up with a dark stone.

Then your eyes will widen like a child's,
your breath held, perhaps forever,
your futile efforts focused on squeezing by
the dark stone, creeping through the black door.

They say, that sometimes when he read,
striking out for some strange town in his small car,
he'd swing by the lake for his neighbour,
his close friend, who was wise on many things.
And if, during the course of the long night of laying bare,
he was cornered by someone intent on draining him,
or calling him friend,
or revealing where they felt his last attempt
had faltered, or gone wrong,
he would catch his neighbour's eye,
introduce him as his mentor,
who would then hold forth on the many quirks in nature:
the changing face of ivy,
how ducks loved sedge,
the link between the Concorde and the swan
– and he, himself, the writer,
would ease away and mingle
or stand quietly by the window,
taking in the hum of generation,
the hush of the lake,
the way sunlight pinpointed through a canopy of leaves.

TEACHER

Travelling back from Limerick that day
when one wrong turn threw you off;
the chatting classmates safely in the back,
the sunshine shining a light for you,
the houses growing larger, more secluded
and apart until even the children noticed,
your persistence pressing you forward
into another world, your restless charges
knowing you were lost at least, or worse,
the road narrowing until to turn back
became the least viable of the options
and the children fell into a game,
spotting Boston on a roadside post,
pointing inwards towards the uplands,
Kilfenora becoming California, Inagh,
a mad woman or a bottomless lake
becoming China, the children chanting:
Peking, Nanking, Shandong, Shanghai,
you introducing with Tiananmen, Taiwan
and Chairman Mao, until the villages
ceased altogether and the rough gravel
chattered to the tyres, Lemenah Castle
alone, above a stone valley, prayed
the children towards wonderment, time
fading to the margins of the stone,
the low sun a portal in the west.

BEACH IN A BOX

That final week you craved the beach:
wishing infinities of sand between your toes,
shells sharp on your calloused soles,
pebbles lodging in your soft knees,
kneeling to imbibe the salt taste,
easing the seaweed between your lips,
gripping the nipple-full bubbles in your teeth,
drinking up the carrageen richness of the sea.

The forcing conflict pinned you to your bed,
victory re-defined with every hour
until all of us could see the battle lost,
and a friend travelled from the coast,
a cigar-box of beach his chosen gift:
the sand slipping through your fingers,
blue pebble-tears in your swollen grip,
a shell held to your ear, your terror
hushed in the sibilant push of the sea.

Off the Game

No poem today mister poet
too far off the game not in the race
out in the outfield off the pace
nothing coming my way on the wind
no heat in the sun no sun
no faces on the people I met
no lives to be seen or guessed at
no space no easing into the groove
no sudden moves
no good running off the ball
no clear call
no nod to the open net
no good get
too many fluffed passes
too many dropped balls
way too many late calls
too much spin too little slice
too much bend
too high in the end
too wide of the target
too close to call
too loose on the bends
too tight to the wall
too clear of the bar
too low by far
too far to the right
too hurt by the night
too tense too tight
too tied down too locked in
no grip no win
no way home no poem.

BLACK EARTH

Tschernosem? – she guessed, bending close
to the black soil of a north Mayo bog,
expecting the fine-grained, wind-blown
loess of her native steppe, but finding sponge,
water-filled, a lung flooded, the land
unsteady, the shiver-thin grass-coat saving
nothing. Unlike the darkened earth,
chernaya zemlya, of her homeland, porous,
fine-grained, unstratified, but pushing up food,
making families, pushing them out to earn,
to carry back, blowing across maps,
picking mushrooms in the tunnels, saving
everything. All the pickers from her village,
sending their morsels back, like the loess,
fine-grained, yes, but bringing it together,
until, and here she smiled, under pressure
it bonded, was known to stand intact in cliffs.

HUNGRY WOMAN

For nigh on two years, she said,
she'd fasted on the bones of a handsome man,
wove spells about his tousled head,
enticed him with cooked titbits,
left sweetmeat morsels on his step.
She fed him pointed comments about needs,
spun love lines towards him scrawled
on parchment, tattooed in her own blood,
stood naked before the full moon, calling him,
her arms outstretched like the diviner's rod.
Pulling him towards the centre of her earth,
his arms binding her, his scent
driving everything from her heart but him.
Her cries through the deaf estate,
echo off the heedless walls, skim
the blind windows, stitch through the parked cars;
scratch on his door, scratch on his door ...

DERNIER CRI

Back years ago, my sainted aunt
(when saints were still in vogue)
took all our years of cottage ware:
old jugs, crock jars, black metal tongs
deep wardrobes of stained pine, and
consigned it all to the farthest shed
to gather there in the dusty dark
enmeshed in cobwebs, soot stained, dead.

Then in their place she bought 'all new'
bright Pyrex bowls and clear glass plates,
formica tops and padded metal chairs,
built-in wardrobes of highly buffed veneer
to dazzle in the new white light and
amaze the neighbours coerced to 'call for tea'.

Brass oil lamps, lasts, white pitchers, ewers,
delph basins cracked, all crossed the yard
to languish in the crowded, edge-ways dark.
Even our statues found their way across:
peeling Marys, a headless Child of Prague
Blessed Martin, suffering from a skin defect
and many glowing Sacred Hearts
with their inner love exposed.

Today we toil to salvage from this throve
like some old-time election crowd
we count our casting votes: this lamp will suit,
that iron too and the deep gilt plates should
fit in well with the stressed wash-stand
with basin cracked, the pitcher and the ewer.

Free-standing wardrobes, re-elected
are back against the bedroom walls
all bare again of built-ins and veneers.
Each time I cross, the treasure is reduced,

some artefact, a speck from off the stack,
so that less and less remains, except for
broken plates, the woodwormed frames
and peeling virgins, homeless, on their backs.

That Face

It was never a nightmare – no,
something more magical than that
– you, Michael, on piano,
the thinning hair,
your heavy glasses perched,
turning to the band with a
run, calling up a tune,
and on guitar that man from the daytime
soap, fingers flexed,
while the separated mother we both know
surprised me there
behind the drums, running ripples
through the skins,
and you, Margaret, at the mike
and not a hospital in sight,
striking up some jazz classic,
all wild hair and attitude,
while at the back,
that fifth face I cannot
bring to mind,
no matter how I shift
through the angles of the light,
nor the instrument,
something curved, sharp-edged,
of metal maybe
– strumming, watchful,
trying hard to be part
of the scene, pretending
to hold the tune.

FIXATION

Jimmy was the *go-man* at all the big jobs,
spinning the stick: *stop-go, stop-go*.
Sometimes he assumed outrageous stances
to pass the time for the motorists and himself.
Other days he felt he was the stop-man mostly,
but that was just the downside of the job.
Later he took to halting all the traffic,
the curving length of Larchfield Drive,
commuters coming to a dead stop,
Jimmy motionless in his yellow strip,
while his wife reversed, brow-knotted
to the narrow space beyond the shed
where Jimmy stored his spinning stick
since she'd banned it from the house
after the Christmas carol-singer incident.
When she was away at her sisters
he would regulate the bathroom traffic, his
children came to know of entry and egress,
he called time by the bolted bathroom door,
rigid stance, sign in hand, jacket bright,
the go-stick spinning to the morning news.
The night she found it resting by their bed,
a stripped-down Jimmy, in his yellow strip,
became a defining moment in their marriage.
Now he drives a forklift; things are on the up.

CARVING A SHEELA NA GIG

I coveted your job then:
the sun full-on,
the back garden hushed,
the blackbird in the thorn-bush,
all angled head and locked eye
at the tip-tip of your chisel,
breath-puff and dust-blow.
Her lips easing from the sandstone,
every sinew strained,
her breasts meeting the light,
you bending close between her thighs,
finding every crease of her
in the pressed block,
chisel-tapping the soft stone,
giving her shape: rock-icon,
woman-blessing, her ancestors high
on church gables long before the doors
narrowed, long before the burka,
even long before the veil.

RECIPE FOR COOKING A HAT

Having removed the head, steep the hat
in a portly marinade of Spanish wine,
add a sprinkling of dusty herbs,
even the chaff of storage jars will do;
they carry their own delicate scent.

Take any vegetables to hand and slice them,
leaving the skins intact for texture;
they enrich the flavour too. Use whatever
you have, there are no ordinary vegetables,
but add chillies to burn a pathway to your gut
and a blood orange to give it zest.

Stir the lot with a great spatula, see the rich felt
darken, the sweatband curl to a bacon texture,
watch the maker's label peel away, the ink leech
into the swirling mess: Darkday and Son, Milliners
since 1833. Observe the matted whole loosen,
strip apart, to become like strands of river hair.

Let it rest a day or so to absorb the goodness,
then source a suitable utensil: this may come
easy to hand, be offered by friends or materialise
on your door-step in the small hours,
a snide note attached urging caution.
Take that utensil and scour it 'til it shines,
seal it with the best oil you have, something Italian
with a tincture of the sun, ease it to the heat
until a blue smoke rises to sting your eyes.

Then you pour the steeping mess, carefully,
feel as kisses of heat hiss from the metal pot,
your breath caught in a moment of lurid taste,
watch wide-eyed as bubbles form, in ones at first,

then in whole families with shared skins, clinging,
and you stir, throwing in new light, the essence
staining the spatula the colour of spilt blood.

And when it's cooked they'll gather about you
at the oak table, with raucous cries and jibes,
reminders of how you came to this, taunting,
watching as you swirl the glutinous mess,
ladling it into a deep bowl: an elderly
heirloom's best, with a cracked glaze.
Then you spoon it 'til it's gone,
spoon it quickly while they pound
the table, gloating as you force it down,
feeling its eelgrass slither, the chillies heat
giving you heart as you swallow and swallow,
dragging victory and maybe legend from your loss.

COLD FEVER

For seven years I've searched
for the final film we'd seen
before the end of winter,
the final winter as we knew,
even then; you felt it was a watershed.

Now I've found it again, 'Cold Fever':
a Japanese commemorating his parents'
death, set in wintertime, in Iceland;
whiteness without end, driving blind,
snow swirling; drifts on all the paths,

throwing the protagonists off course,
roads hidden and treacherous underfoot,
fears everywhere and the need to cling.
But you liked the light shots best,
sunrises on towers of burning ice;

the true cold of a no-holds-barred winter.
You loved the honey-run of light
along the ice-fields, geysers bursting
unannounced, the exhaled hiss of steam,
the side-by-side, hot and cold sensation

of windblown candles burning on the floes,
their souls carried over in that pale light,
a son's prayers to a chosen god,
a libation poured in the torrent;
the unstoppable race to the ocean.

PICTURING THE FROG

You chased him around the garden,
through the rock-pool with its copper heron,
bird-shadow puckering his green skin.

Through the rockeries, imitating his hop, hop,
prodding him warily with a straw,
across the gravel beds of heather,

forcing him to excesses of hopping,
watching him scrabble over the stones,
his climber's legs gripping the lichen,

his webbed toes mysterious to you,
his slow-blink eyes protruding
as he strained to jump,

his pulsing throat fluttering until, finally
he held his pose, refused to hop another inch
– which was when you snapped him,

froze him in his digital frame,
from where he stares out, captured, transfixed
his almost human look of resignation

somehow familiar to us all.

Away Too Long

Reading to a foreign audience
the poet was seized with an unrequited urge
to speak in his own tongue,
knowing there was little chance that a word
would float back from the upturned wave of faces,
all of them keen for the poetry they knew,
unwilling to stretch beyond the lines
which had drawn them there.

But his chest grew heavy with the need,
his throat filling up with it:
the glottal snap of the word for love,
a whispered breeze as his lover spoke it,
the lull of the fleeting moon over his town,
the strain of the river wrestling towards the tide,
the wish of the tide embracing it.

He focussed on a woman in the front row,
the stone at her throat like a January sky,
tasted 'Eanair' on his tongue.
Saw a man cloud his eyes like a hawk
before it drops, felt 'seabhac' on his lips.
Raised his gaze to the ceiling to focus,
saw a spider cast off from a shaded web,
craved for the need to speak that word,
but could not remember it and realized
then that he'd been away too long.
He returned his attention to the page,
left the spider dangling there unspoken,
tried to continue, the spider teasing out
a silken thread across his vision,
his mind struggling with the line.

Signing afterwards in the crowded room,
he felt its nimble stalks teasing him,
its name astray in his mind's eye,

his pen a spider crawl across the page
until with the final stroke, 'damhán alla'
came to him as he took the organiser's hand,
confessed he had to leave, had a plane to catch.

HOW ORDINARY HE LOOKED

There were two schools of thought
on skipping through the school gates:
some inmates eased the head first,
dropped the shoulder and followed,
the body sliding between the bars,
while others took the walking route,
feet first, then the torso, with the head
bringing up the rear, the ears protected,
eyes shut tight. Some got wedged
halfway, requiring assistance or even force
to get them through, or ease them back.
Kevin got 'the stocks' for five minutes once
until the threat of Dim Daly's size nines
brought him to a mad frenzy of freedom,
his glasses awry, both his temples grazed.
Bighead! Daly screamed as Kevin popped,
just avoiding the aimed kick, Daly jailed
by his own girth, or by his 'magnitude'
as Mister Malone put it to Daly's mother
the day he became fully jammed, with
the whole school gathered to witness
the bully trapped. How ordinary he looked,
his muscles useless, his heavy boots askew,
his mother telling him how this was nothing
compared to what his father would give him,
if the firemen freed him and she got him home.

LESSON

At eighty-seven, I thought her lessons were long past,
her mind confused by many things,
her hands no longer steady,
her eyes elsewhere in the room.

Unlike the stormy day when I was nine,
a long-forgotten errand resting in the drain,
while I fished a tin lid and sailed it
on river-rain towards Holohans,
all time forgotten, the bread adrift
and puddled, her voice calling me,
her concerned voice, and then her scolding one.
Like my own today when I found her,
long overdue, the loaf discarded,
poking at a roadside flower
with her bent stick; saying it was a sign
of bad luck to flower so early,
whispering to me how 'men would come'.
Urging me 'to hide the guns'.

THE MIRROR THING

You're doing that mirror thing again,
looking just beyond where you stand
until you're in the background
as people will see you,
becoming a stranger to yourself.
Then you do the 'push-in',
moving closer to the glass
to see yourself in a newer light
turning through the angles,
gauging how well you look
to you, as you tilt your head
forward for the deep-eye look
and back to check the neck-
line, touching nothing but the hair.
It's a miracle in movement,
a journey taken,
all those images trapped,
references stored away, before
the final turn and the long look
back to scan the line
and only then do you ask:
'Well, how do I look?'
And I manage 'fine, fine'.

Second Curse

I wish you not here, your time collapsed into itself,
your breath cut short to your first inhaled cry,
that intake trapped in your parents' moan,
that moan travelling backwards
to their mistimed orgasm;
their broken breath reduced to a fatal slip
causing them never to mate:
your spawning a cancelled wavelet,
one ripple skipped on a broad lake.

STILTWALKER

Before that day she looked up:
to her sisters, her dad, the teachers.
Even mum, her friend was up there somewhere
pointing out the giant rules of not running,
not looking, not everything, not anything.
Then he came walking with his giraffe
gait, on his spindle legs,
she knew his wig was false, but bending down
he lifted her into the great parade.
The red-nosed clown tooted his whistle,
waved an admonishing finger as they waltzed,
the stuffed teddy-bears cried 'No', the unicyclist
hid his eyes, the dancers tapped faster,
but she held on. Dad's hand was raised,
his eyes large, his bald patch visible,
mum's mouth a startled O.
Her sisters, witch-nosed, both pouted,
but she clung on, up there, looking
above the cloudy bar-room windows,
into bedrooms, wardrobes with hatboxes
stacked, the church steeple appeared
shorter, the parked cars all flat,
the stiltwalker humming that silly tune,
the crowd looking up until he lowered her
back to her parents, back to her big sisters,
down to earth, her family all cut down to size.

SPRING

A rumour of green along the branches,
an orrery of birds,
the gainsayer of winter whispers
through the housing estate.

THE PROPERTIES OF WATER

The 'old ones' feared there was a god in water,
would never hold its pulling stare too long.
Though they fished their lives beyond the flaggy shore
they refused to hear of swimming;
wore coarse wool for warmth and for weight
to draw them down should their canvas craft disintegrate.

The day my father's friends took Horgan's boat,
launched it on the bobbing, sunny waves,
plugged the one small hole with a green sod,
went rowing towards the island, all in fun,
never guessing how clay would wear and melt
'til they saw the salty oozing through the scraw.

How Dolan stamped his foot too hard,
drove down to keep the seeping ocean out,
his leg sinking to the groin in the blackened sea,
how his two friends rowed, praying, 'Haul!, Haul!'
with the god of water gnawing at their toes,
Dolan wedged between this life and the next.

Black Randal's hooker plucked them from the brink,
their boat just brimming, the oarsmen sagging, still.
'Long' Dolan never faced the sea again,
would talk of the pull, how his leg was held
in a powerful vice, how Randal's crew
fought tug-of-war to free him from its hold.

Years later on the shore, my father shared
how Dolan had moved soon after into town,
afraid of the water's constant lonely call,
how he had married in outside, reared children,
working deep in a black hole, shovelling grain,
or coal, where he might never meet the sea again.

He would seldom ever cross a city bridge,
wove zigzag paths to work, down lanes,
through alleyways, cycling fast by gravel tracks,
in and out of side streets, always avoiding water
and if he had to cross a bridge, he did it quickly,
pedalling flat and staring straight ahead.

Sometimes the fear would still become too much
and his hurried course would shake, vibrate,
then he would scream to the circling gulls
trying to drown the ocean's pulling hiss:
'By Christ, you haven't got me yet'.
Difficult in a land as waterlogged as this.

WORN DOWN

For days the wind has blown,
whip-sands blast my windows,
turning the grey glass opaque.

My vision's blurred;
out there on the sea's edge,
the dunes are stripped back;
serrated layers peeled away,
worn down and down,
to expose the skeletal shoulders,
skull and the humming ribcage
of a man, sea-things crawling
his ragged cavities.

This morning his arm's free,
released from the dunes' grip,
his stick-thin finger beckons.

NOVEMBER DAYS

The children are cutting arcs in the back garden,
they push off from the far wall, a shrapnel
of bodies through the evening light,
their eyes filled with tears in the biting wind.
The smallest one stands and waits as they weave
towards him, the object being to catch
one of them before they can reach the shelter
of the gable-end.

He waits, skinny legs splayed, he knows
their game, they'll try to confuse him,
string dizziness in his eyes. They step-out,
accelerate, slow deliberately, hesitate,
pick a slot. But he waits, makes his selection,
races after one of them, his hand
outstretched, misses; the bigger boy
forced into broader arcs, curves building
off each other, the tiny one reaching,
straining another arc from the tall kid's
pumping dance as the small one lunges

one last time, barely misses a flap
of tracksuit hem, overshoots and spins,
a forced smile widening on his pinched face
as they hit the gable wall, throws his arms
high to their cries of 'Home! Home! Home!

WARSHOW

We know they're out there,
somewhere and always,
so in the days before the big day,
we listen,
for the faintest cutting of the ether,
up there, almost beyond our hearing,
and when the bumble-bee hum
of the first helicopter,
scout, outrider,
rumbles across our sky, saying,
'look at me, so slow, so awkward,
and what harm can looking do?' we listen,
while high up,
there's still the faintest sound
of whetted metal slicing through the air.

SHEDDING SKIN

I long to shed my skin, pin it
on a burning rock to shrivel
and harden to a husk.
To take that husk and grate it
to a dust so fine the wind
will whip it across the shore,
spread it to the winds,
while I step out, new-born,
smooth and purged of your
impurities, your lizard touch.

Winter

A halogen sun cuts low across the playing fields,
industrial rain sweeps up the bay,
in silhouette, the housing estate is a ragged cliff.
By his gate an old man clings to the top bar,
his garden a gethsemane of dead leaves.

ELECTION-TIME, SALTHILL

Along the promenade the candidates
hang from lampposts,
their over-sized portraits confirming
everything we might need
in the rosy new future
they've planned for us.
The posters cost small Euros each,
or even less if printed in China.
Globalized, we don't trust
their out-sized, air-brushed smiles,
their gladiator eyes, even when
the wind whips in from the Atlantic,
bending the posters in half,
showing us how the politicians
strain their backs for us,
break their necks.

GOD IN TENNIS

Relaxing after some match or other
when things had gone quite well;
you meeting the ball with ease;
spin befuddling the opponent's mind,
we got to talking about the nature
of things and the finite drip of time.
Tom claiming Hollywood owed him
one hundred and ten minutes, time
he could never claim back, sitting
in the darkness with some director's
big mistake. How the absence of irony
was our biggest loss, how we, the bungling
masses, were the final judges and soldiers
eating each other's brains was now considered
an aberration we must all take the slack for
should the hitch knot slip.

You out there keeping your head still
focusing in on the rolling toss,
the flexing kick of the yellow ball,
the minute shift of grip, your breath
held and the hipbone easing 'round,
your shoulder cocked, accelerating towards
your eye, the ball suspended there,
a perfect orb, with the staring nap erect,
before your punch launches it beyond
your opponents reach, to send it kicking
in the sand, sticking in the fence;
staying in the game, longing, like all of us,
for the attempted perfection of yet another shot.

OFF THE MOTORWAY

At four am when the nightmare came:
his hands about her straw-thin neck,
her eyes bulging like a grounded trout,
her body writhing under him,
leaving him erect in the blurred blackness,
he left their sundered bed,
relieved that it was just a dream.

He packed a small bag by the mirror light,
the glow showing his terror sweats,
black smears like punches by his eyes,
then he drove to the Silver Strand to see the sun rise,
slept for three days on the cramped backseat,
spent those days just staring at the waves,
but could not throw himself into the sea.

Later he sold the car for cash,
removed the tent they'd shared on a summer hike,
and walked along the shoreline heading east,
until one day, with the water to his right,
he eased off the busy road,
three steps down to a hidden shelf of grass,
pitched the tent and let the world pass him by.

He lived on very little while he healed,
the world to his back, just off the motorway,
the traffic rushing, like a wave, above his head.

HISTORY LESSON

When the sea punched through into steerage
and the pinched souls there crushed each other
underfoot to reach the hatches and saw under-
standing in the eyes of those they crushed,
the thugs had already crawled over anything
which moved, gouged heel-grips towards
the heavens, the masts scraping the cataract
dark as they climbed, up and up, away
from the crawling decks, the lifeboats lost,
away from the milling masses, the numbed
children, away from the whitewashed rocks,
the rigging slick with silt, the only fear that
the bilge rats climbing with them, their chatter
all around them in the black, would slash
their flesh as they climbed, never guessing
that when they tipped into the crows-nest
and perceived safety they would sink
into a depth of bristle-fur, bathe in rat flesh,
feel the nip and stab of needle teeth, clear
affinity with the squirm of vermin muscle,
their crimson pin-points lighting up the dark.

WINDFALLS

Today I spread the last of the autumn apples,
cider-sweet under the bare trees: a harvesting
for the hungry birds, who stand
in the brown gold, almost mesmerised,
picking at the soft flesh, a wary eye
on the kitchen window, where I watch them.
I imagine their distrust of a free meal.
For them, where is the catch?

About the Author

James Martyn is from Galway and is a member of the Talking Stick Workshop. His work has been broadcast on RTÉ and BBC Radio and he won the Listowel Writers' Week Originals short story competition. He was shortlisted for a Hennessy Award in 2006, for the Francis Mac Manus Award in 2007 and 2008 and the William Trevor International Short Story Competition in 2007.

Acknowledgements

Thanks to the editors of the following publications where some of these poems first appeared: *The Cúirt Journal*, *West 47*, *Books Ireland*, *Crannóg*, *The Sunday Tribune*, *The Stinging Fly*, *The SHOp*. Thanks also to Galway City Council and James C. Harrold, Arts Officer, for receipt of a bursary to the Tyrone Guthrie Centre at Annaghmakerrig where some of these poems were revised and written. Thanks to The Talking Sticks Workshop for signing the adoption papers.

'Reverse Chronologist' is for Maurice Ward.
'Teacher' is for Maura Kelly.
'Beach in a Box' is dedicated to the memory of Mary Parvin, New York.
'Carving a Sheela na Gig' is for Pat Bracken.
'Cold Fever' is dedicated to the memory of Anne Kennedy.
'The Mirror Thing' is for Martha.